LEARNING to SWIM

a collection of poems on postpartum depression

JM Lee

Copyright © 2026 by Jessica Gonzales / JM Lee

All rights reserved. This book or any portion thereof may not be reproduced or used in any manner whatsoever without the express written permission of the publisher except for the use of brief quotations in a book review.

This book is not a substitute for medical advice. If you or someone you know is struggling, please talk to a medical professional.

ISBN 979-8-9917822-4-1
Book Cover by GetCovers

For more information, visit www.jmlee.info

LEARNING to SWIM

a collection of poems on postpartum depression

JM Lee

DEDICATED TO

everyone who kept me alive
in those early months postpartum

to the family who helped

the husband who loved unconditionally

the friends who showed up

and the medical professionals who saved me

I don't know if I'd be here today without you

Thank you

TABLE OF CONTENTS

A note from the author..7

Introduction..10

Drowning...18

Learning...138

Calmer Waves...206

A NOTE FROM THE AUTHOR

I am not a medical professional. This book should not substitute any medical care or advice that you would receive from a real doctor. This is simply me sharing my experience, hoping that it can help someone feel seen.

When I first became a mom, I didn't realize how common it was to feel the weight of all of these new responsibilities. The more women I talk to, the more I realize that we're not alone. However, society tells us to smile and just enjoy motherhood. But that's hard when your head is loud and your heart cares too much.

The first half of this book is dark. It's a deep-dive into my toughest moments, and the feelings I felt during that time. It was hard to write, and even harder to edit. As someone who ***does not call herself a poet,*** I hope you'll be gentle with my words. I hope you understand that this is just one way in which I processed my emotions coming into motherhood. I never intended on publishing this, but here we are.

At the end of the day, there is light at the end of the tunnel, and it does get better. Please know that you're never alone. And if you're ever feeling overwhelmed or like you may hurt yourself or others, please call **988**, **the Suicide and Crisis hotline,** and seek immediate medical attention. Above all, talk to your loved ones.

YOU ARE NOT ALONE, AND YOU ARE LOVED.

CONTENT WARNINGS:
- Depression & Anxiety
- Suicidal Ideation
- Body Dysmorphia
- Blood

INTRODUCTION

TWO YEARS DROWNING

I sit alone
on the eve of my son's
second birthday

That smile
Those rocky blue eyes
Little feet that never stop moving
Dancing along the ground

I should be happy
Should be thankful
Should cry tears of joy until
My heart could explode from happiness

After all,
I've made it this far...

But I can't
Somehow I'm distraught
I feel jaded

So many little memories lost
The monster that is motherhood

That stole my baby
Stole those precious moments
Of counting tiny toes
And snuggling away the woes of growing up

She stole my baby
This darkness inside
This voice that screams
You're not good enough

Not loving enough
Not patient enough
Not strong enough

Never.
Enough.

She stole my baby and
all I have is the pictures and
videos on my phone
as reminders
of who he was in the beginning

Who I used to be

The monster that overtook me
The fear that washed over me
Consumed me
Told me I wasn't fit to be a mother
That he'd be better off with another
Because no one in this whole wide world
deserves to be raised
by someone as low as me

They tell you it's normal,
your doctors and friends
It's normal to mourn your past
The life that at last slipped
through your fingers
like quick sand
gone before you could even blink

1 in 5 women have postpartum depression
Does no one stop to think
Why that number is so high?
And yet all they say is...

It's normal.
This is motherhood.

So now
On the eve of my son's second birthday
I will mourn

I will look through the photographs and videos
I will count the smallest of details
Listen to every little giggle

I will cry
And sob
And scream
And be angry

Because I don't remember those days
Postpartum depression robbed me of my baby
Took those precious first months
Away
Like a thief

And all I can do,
Is
Hit Play
Swipe
Hit play
Swipe again
And cry

FACT

They estimate nearly 50% of women
experience this
without a proper diagnosis

My fact:
Despite that number
I will still feel alone
and assume I'm the only one

An even truer fact:
Depression is not synonymous with failure
It's is synonymous with learning
how to be a mom

ULTRASOUND PHOTOS

The only thing
still connecting me to you
To the squiggly little worm
you once were

To the little jelly bean that
wiggled in my tummy

The tiny feet that
pushed against my skin
like an alien
in walls too tight

Kicking my bladder
and almost
making me pee myself

The little soccer player doing
cartwheels
and flipping off the monkey bars
that were my ribs

...are these ultrasound pictures

SOMETIMES I THINK

It hurts more knowing that
I was drowning
for months

Wasn't myself
for months

Wanted to die
for months

And no one noticed

Life went on
and I felt more alone than ever
and no one noticed

Sometimes I think
I hate myself more
for hiding it so well

I can't blame others
when I wouldn't tell them the truth

When I lied through my teeth
Smiled and said *I'm enjoying motherhood*

When in fact
I was drowning

HOSPITAL TALK

You're so lucky
she says

I didn't get to eat at all for 12 hours
the other adds

I'm sending snapchats when I should be
relaxing and focusing on
the contractions that threatened
to crumble me to my knees

But instead
I'm sending my friends
videos of me eating
sloppy Joe's and
hospital coleslaw

Wondering when this
child will finally
come out of me

BLEEDING

If you want an epidural
You have to get it right now

The words swim around my head
like fish in the sea

But I'm scared
I don't really know
if I'm prepared for the
level of pain I'm about to be in

When the pushing finally starts
I tear

Stitches—you'll need them
she says
Operates on me like
I'm a sandwich at a deli

My head is woozy
Mind muddled
Eyes fuzzy

I can't see two feet in front of me
That won't change for some time

No one tells you that you won't
remember your child's birth
as they take him from your arms
put him under a light

I can't even hear if he's crying
    He needs to go to the NICU
    Just for a little while

I won't be coherent enough
to notice

Won't be aware enough
to know that I'm even still alive

In the clouds
that's where I am
as they pump me full of fluids to
keep me from drowning

GREEN BEANIE

All the babies
Who visit the
NICU
Get one

A little hand-knitted beanie

Green
like the grassy fields on
soft spring days

Green like the innocence of the
little creature
squirming in my hands

What if I break him?
What if I hurt him?
Is that sound normal?

GOD,

Look at those eyes

To see your creation
moving outside of you

is to know
the true meaning
of love

VIDEOS

I'm glad someone took a video
of me holding him
right after he was born

I'm panting
feeling blocked pain

He's more purple than I remember
Those tiny cries
His and mine

My baby, I say

    Dad, do you want to cut the cord?

Why is he so purple?

My husband looks so calm
Eyes glistening
but not crying
only proud

Full of love

BINKI

this video of him
on our first day home

A Binki in his mouth
bigger than his own face

I'm wide awake,
I croon
I'm not going to sleep!

I remember this
barely
but I do

Those first few days home
the unyielding exhaustion

The way your cry startled me awake
in a complete panic

Is something wrong?
Did I do something
wrong?

But you're just hungry
or need a change
I know this
but why does my heart
never stop pounding?

BREAST IS BEST

That's what they say
The guilt
that tells you no matter what
you need to keep trying

formula
is the devil
it'll kill your baby if you let it!

> *You don't want*
> *to ruin your child*
> *do you?*

But what happens
when your boobs don't work?

Friday we go home
by sunday he won't stop screaming
by monday
he's lost so much weight we
may have to check him back
into the hospital

But all on his own
> *You can't stay with him if that's the case*
You want to take me from my baby?

But god, that means I could sleep for a change
but that means my baby
is away from me!

Breast is best
but my boobs don't work

How the fuck do I
feed him when the
body that was created to maintain him
won't play along

Wont eat enough
to feed enough
to produce enough

Always.
Not.
Enough.

So we'll try formula.
I guess…

beast is best
but sometimes
best
is surviving

And that's okay

Too bad there won't be enough of that
either

10 PM

sleeping

11 pm
screaming

12 am
feeding
try to breastfeed
try to pump
end up formula feeding anyway

He doesn't take my nipple
Is it me?
Does he just not want me?

1 am
diaper change

2am
now time to wash
bottles and pump parts

How much time do I have left to sleep
before we repeat?

3am
now get some sleep

4 am
crying
the baby or me?
who knows at this point

I'm so tired
I want to quit
but this is a life sentence
one I've longed for

When will I sleep again?
God I want to quit
but I won't
because
you're worth every tear

NIGHT-TIME SCARIES

Every night
when the sun sets
and the moon comes out to play

My stomach turns to knots
my heart begins to race
my head floods with worry

Every night
I dread the idea
of trying to sleep
because I know
I'll be up in 2 hours

Every night
I wish
I could just get a full night's rest

TWINKLE, TWINKLE

Little star
How I wonder who you are

Will I ever sleep again?
When will these tears end?

Twinkle, twinkle
Little star
How I wonder who you are

Little baby
In my arms

Tightly swaddled
Safe and warm

Twinkle twinkle
Little star
How I wonder who you are
~ 2 am thoughts

FORMULA SHORTAGE

That's what the news says
A major plant that makes the stuff
shuts down
millions of cans of formula
recalled

Shit...
maybe formula does kill your baby
but I can't produce any milk

These stupid
fucking
boobs
are **useless**

Why have them if they don't even work?
the guilt eats at me
as I drive from store to store

I can't find formula
can't make anything to feed you
never have I felt like a bigger failure

I've failed to
provide you
with the basic necessities of life
already
and you're only a few weeks old

I'm drowning in a sea of desperation
other moms
with weary eyes
roaming empty shelves
worried
wasting so much money
trying to find what's right for you

We're all on the same boat
and all of us are
sinking

A VIDEO OF HIM SLEEPING

That's what I'm watching now

It's starts as a cute one
He's napping
I assume I wanted to capture
the little facial expressions he makes

the smile
the frown

But then I remember why I took this one
I mention we're waiting for
a refill
acid reflux medicine

He starts to huff
starts to breathe sharp
and then it stops

His breath just

s t o p s

I put my hand on his chest
tell the camera
explain that he's not breathing

That he didn't do this when he was on a medicine
I don't remember giving in the first place
And again...
not breathing.

No wonder I was terrified
No wonder I still cried months after he was born

They don't warn you how terrifying it'll be
to watch your little miracle sleep
but stop breathing

TO THE VISITORS

Don't take the baby from her

She wants to see you
    (or maybe she doesn't)
but she definitely doesn't want you to take her baby

Do the dishes
Run a load of laundry
Vacuum her floors

But don't separate her
when she's trying to understand
how to make this all work

Just be there
Don't push
Let her know she's not alone

But don't take her baby

NOISES

whip out my phone
record him again

this is probably the 7th time
today alone

send the video to my bestie

Is this normal?
That noise he's making?
The way he gulps air like that?

> *Calm down,*
> *I'm sure he's fine*
> *But maybe send the video to your doctor*
> *Just in case*

Just in case what?
Is he okay?
Is my baby okay?
Am I okay?

Why will no one tell you
that the scariest part of being a mother
can be your own brain?

DRIVING

No one tells you
how scary it is
to drive
with your heart
detached
in the back seat
of the car

hoping that
some man-made carrier
will protect him
if you mess up

PACK AND PLAY

It's time for a visit
Where?
I don't even remember anymore

baby crying
mom weeping
now screaming
dogs running away

If I could hulk smash
this stupid
    f u c k i n g
plastic
    piece
of
    S H I T
I would

Who makes things like this
for new mothers?
It's like they want me
to hit my breaking point

I WORRY SOMETIMES

that he'll blame himself
this little life I've created
read this and think that he
was the reason why

I hope you know it's not your fault
It never was or could be

Mommy's brain
likes to see mountains
where there's only pebbles
and oceans
where there's a few
tear drops

She may be drowning
but don't you worry, baby

She'll learn how to swim

JEANS

No one
and I mean
no one

warns you how
painful
it'll be to wear jeans again

FIRST TIME OUT

in weeks
a local festival
walking through the streets,

Baby bundled in layers of blankets
Its April
It's nice out
But a little cold

Did I pack enough diapers?
Is he warm enough?

Why are jeans so uncomfortable?

My body
hadn't slimmed down like some
said it would

When will my body feel like mine again?

WHEN WILL MY HEART

no longer
pound in my throat
sending cascading waves
of panic
through my body

Nothing is wrong
and yet somehow
it feels like everything
will never be okay again

I don't want to be here
don't want to be seen
why is it that
your own mind can be so mean?

GUMMY SMILE

When I look at this picture
I don't remember the pain

Mental
Physical

I see your joy
for life
and whatever stupid face
I was probably making
to make you laugh

I see your infectious glee
and it makes my heart warm
that even while I was drowning
for even just a few moments

I was drowning
in love

FACES AND NOISES

That's what I see
when I watch this video
you're a few weeks old

We're snuggled in bed
I look tired

Not just tired
But

T
    I
  R
E
    D

The bags under my eyes say it all
my eyes barely slit open
trying to stay awake

    Don't fall asleep with the baby in your arms

But what if he won't sleep in
his crib alone?

But that button nose
the closed eyes
the little bumps on your face
with the minutes just passing by

Tiny coos
and little sighs

What I wouldn't give
to go back
and once again
relive those times

MOTHER'S GROUP

When I was pregnant
I was part of a
mother's group

Me and three other moms
all talking about anything
that was going wrong

Now that you're here
you come with me to meet them all

One of them,
the doctor
who will save my life
in just a few short days

I see myself in that photo
disingenuous smile
forced
like someone held a gun to my head
and said
    "You have to be happy"

This is your job
you're not allowed to struggle
you're not allowed
to show your true emotions

Not allowed to feel the pain
the way your heart breaks
remembering who you were before

washing baby bottles for the millionth time
that day alone

You asked for this
you wanted to be a mother
Why are you so surprised?

Now that you find out
it's harder than you thought it would be

Be grateful
Be thankful
Don't you dare regret your decision

Mind you
no one ever said these
words to me aloud

I heard them in my heart
like a loud-speaker
crying the words of society

While they all smile,
nod,
and tell me how
beautiful he is
and how lucky I am

I LOVE YOU

with every fiber of my being
every bone in my body
every ounce of my blood

I would burn cities for you
move mountains
for you

But I don't want to be a mom
right now...

How do I explain this
to someone
whose never wanted to
rip open their own skull
and exchange their brain
for a functional one

NO ONE TELLS YOU

how much it hurts
to move your baby
into the next size clothes

MY BODY

hasn't been mine for quite some time
I shared it with him for so long

Now it feels empty with nothing inside
I see the photos
my rolls still there

The pounds I put on
while he was in there
I should love my curves
and tiger stripes
and one day I will

But right then
I just wonder
when I'll feel like
myself
again

LITTLE OLD MAN

That's what you look like
I smile
seeing this photo of you

Fuzzy little head
nose too big for your
newborn face

As you get older
you'll grow into it
but now,

You just look like my little
puppet
ready to keep me awake
for another night

SMILE

your first grin
caught me off guard

I was looking up
down the hall
when my gaze
fell on you again

You were
smiling
the sweetest little face
my heart exploded
and to this day
left without a trace

You took my heart with that smile

This motherhood shit is hard
but you make it worthwhile

You make it
manageable

When I'm ready to drown
you smile now

Remind me that
there's light at the end of the tunnel

And I'll do anything
to see that sweet smirk
across those darling little cheeks

CRYING

wailing
tears rolling down my cheeks

I'm not okay,
I say
between sobs

I can't stop crying
my husband went back to work
now it's just me alone

All day
waiting

For him to get home

Who said I could
take care of him?

Who said I was fit?

What would happen if
I fell down the stairs and

there was no one around?

What if I drop him?

What if I choke
on food or worse
the words that I never dare spoke

I'm not fit to be your mother
you deserve so much better
I know that there's someone out there
who would be better than me

Why am I the monster you
were given to

the beast that cries
and never stops

mourning the life
she had before

I SHOULD BE GRATEFUL

Remember?

I wanted this
Why don't I want this?
Do I really not want this?
or is it just overwhelming?

No one tells you
how you'll speak to yourself after

of the silent battles you'll fight
in your mind

When you can't stand to get up
can't stand to wash another bottle
can't stand to run another load
can't stand to let your nipples
crack and bleed

I hear my internal monologue
like a battle cry
my heart hasn't stopped racing
since we left the hospital

'What if'
pounds in my mind
like war drums
reminding me
that I
will never be
good enough

Maybe I should just leave...

MOTHERHOOD

somehow makes you feel
so wholly complete
and so completely
empty

CAN I BE HONEST WITH YOU?

my husband sits across from me
our son is asleep
finally

I can't stop crying
I haven't *stopped* crying

maybe it's baby blues
maybe it's not

At some point the crying has to stop
my husband is a rational man
can't understand
the pain I'm in

The pain my mind feels
I broke my own heart when
I thought those words

Maybe I should leave?
Did I really think that?
Do I really want to let someone else
raise my baby?

Sadly, yes

Except I don't want to leave
when the realization settles in
that there's worse ways to go

Worse ways to
leave
forever
...
      permanently

But that would be selfish
but maybe just...

maybe to give him a better life
I can't just pack my bags
and leave

My husband and family would judge me
but if I wasn't around for them to
pelt me with their words

I would finally be able to rest...

I'M SO TIRED

I've never felt anything like this

A tiredness so deep
it settles into your bones and really
all you need is rest

But you don't know any better
don't realize that one good night's rest
will help you to tackle the rest
at another time,
another day

But for now
I don't want to pack my things up
and move away.
I want to get my things in order,
and leave forever
in a way that they'll never forgive me for

Because death
seems like the better choice

It's not.

NO ONE TELLS YOU

that motherhood
can make you
consider suicide
thinking it'll give your son
a better life

You couldn't possibly be enough
Right?

Wrong.
but no one warns you...

DOCTOR

Please help me
I know you were
only in charge of my online zoom class

But please

I don't know what to do
I can't stop crying
Can't function
Can't eat
Can't breastfeed my baby

And honestly
can't imagine continuing this life
the way it is

The world feels small
like it's caving in on me

Like I could drown
in the sea of responsibility
in the sea of hormones
that are twisting my mind

turning my into someone
I don't recognize
turning me into darkness that feeds on the light
my son deserves better

If I don't hear back soon,
I'm not sure what I'll do.
please doc
I know you're not *my* doctor
but
what do I do?

PEDIATRICIAN

When you go to the pediatrician,
you have to complete a form
in the first few months

Some for your baby
Some for your mental health
I see the question at the bottom
      Have you considered hurting yourself?

I want to lie
smile and nod
pretend everything's fine

But I tell myself *'no'*
I'll be honest
so when the pediatrician reads over the paper
her eyes widen at the sight of my confession

It's okay, I've already seen my
OBGYN
I've been on Zoloft for a week now and it's
Helping
Slowly

but it doesn't matter.
she just sees what's on the paper

When the appointment
is over
we stand in the waiting room
she hands me a paper and says
loud enough for everyone to hear

> *Here's the number*
> *for the suicide hotline*
> *if you ever feel like you need it*
> *don't hesitate to call*

And I've never wanted to drown
more than I did in that moment

And then later that day,
she'll call CPS
they'll call me asking if I need medical help
it will only solidify in my mind
that I'm a terrible mom

She'll be one of the reasons
I drown for longer than I needed to

DON'T TELL ME I'M OVERREACTING

Every moment
you diminish my thoughts
my worries

which I share with you in confidence
in a moment of desperation
to settle my mind

When you tell me
I'm overreacting

I feel inadequate
like I'm not cut out to do this

like all I can do is overthink
and worry
about when the next shoe will drop

I'VE ALWAYS HATED MY SINGING VOICE

but seeing you smile
and smirk
and coo
when I sing to you
makes my heart happy
and my soul warm

It makes the sleepless nights
worth it all the more

ANOTHER VIDEO

In this one
you're sleeping
finally

Your face flashes from crying
to smiling

I'm not sure what you're dreaming
I wish I could be in your mind
maybe it would be a vacation
from the darkness inside mine
maybe you dream of butterflies
or blocks
or the colorful little books
that make funny noises when you touch them
like crinkling paper

Do you even know what a butterfly is yet?
maybe you dream of bottles of milk
or boobs

I wonder what you're dreaming
while I'm drowning

BABY CARRIER

I have you strapped to my chest
I say you're getting so big
but looking back
you were the tiniest of miracles
that I ever got to hold

YOU THERE,

the reader

You probably think I'm the worst
some evil horrid thing
that would want to kill herself
to escape motherhood

But you don't understand
what it's like unless
you've been there yourself

to be drowning
surrounded by air

the only way up
is by clawing your way through

through the thickness of anxiety
the fog of depression
only to find yourself
one step closer
each day

Without realizing it
you'll breath in
and think

holy shit

I'm still alive.
I made it.

Eventually I won't have to drown anymore

FIRST SHOTS

We're back at that same pediatrician
that little bitch

and today
she gives you your first shot

I remember your cries
they ripped out my insides
I was ready to tear out my own heart
if it meant I
could stop your pain
for even just a moment

No one warns you
how heartbreaking it is
to hear your baby's pain

DO ME A FAVOR

that voice in your head?
the one that screams
I can't do this
I certainly can't do this
forever

When she cries out in your mind,
tell her:
>*it won't be forever*
>*you can't do this forever, sure*
>*because it won't always feel like this*
>*a day will come*
>*and it won't be so hard*
>
>*it may be challenging for different reasons*
>*but it won't feel like you're drowning*
>*I promise*

Recognize that voice in your head
tell her it's okay
tell her you understand her pain

But also remind her,
that it will only last a small season

The waves will cease
and you'll come out on the other side
afloat
wishing you could go back

and do it all again

CRADLE

I miss having you next to me
you're a big two year old now
and I look at old videos
and photos

of when you were my little
shadow
always beside my bed

in your cradle
cooing and sighing
beckoning me to hold you
feed you
love you

You never had to ask twice
I've always loved you
I want that to be clear as day
there was not a moment I didn't love you

even when I didn't love
myself

ANGER

It brews in my chest
I could do it so much faster
Do it my way

Change the diaper
Feed the baby
Make the bottle
Wash the laundry
Cook dinner
Everything

I want things done my way
I want them quick
I want them done right

Why does it feel so impossible
to let someone else
take over for just a moment

So I can rest
So I can breathe

So I can *"relax"*
      What's that like?

Why can't I let go of the anger
that makes me think
I have to do it all alone
all by myself
for it to be done right?

KISSES

I pepper you in them
You're laying under
a baby mobile
looking at colorful circles above you

I lean in
kiss your nose
your tiny voice
coos when I get close

Those sloppy little hands
rubbing your face
without a care

like you can't control them yet
like they have a mind of their own

and your eyes flutter
between me and the colors
and all I can do

is thank the universe
or god

or whoever listens to my internal cries

thank them
that I didn't
leave you
like I wanted to all those weeks ago

I may be drowning
but I'm still here
I'm still your momma
and those tiny giggles
make it all worth it

YOU CAME FROM ME

and yet somehow you'll always be
a dream I worry
I'll one day wake up from
and realize
you weren't real

FLOPPY HEAD

I see videos of me
holding you

You're trying to move your head around
and it's flopping

and I wonder what I was thinking
to let you flail like that

I should've held tighter
What if I'd hurt you?
What if you'd hurt yourself?
Am I even doing this *'mom'*
thing right?

I see videos of you
and all I can do it judge myself

WE FEEL LIKE ROOMMATES NOW

my husband and I
for months we're both just surviving
wishing for sleep
wishing for a break
for a small moment where things feel like
they did before we fell in love
with the tiny terror that keeps us up at night
and cries and cries and cries

I have to make an effort to connect with you
yet I've never felt so alone

no one warns you how much
you'll miss your partner
after becoming parents

BABY CRIES

in this video
I squeeze your cheeks

you're like a baby doll
rubber and make-believe

except you're real
not a doll
flesh and blood

my
flesh and blood

You were just giggling
I say as you begin to cry
I guess you've had enough
of me
for one night

I think I've had enough of me too

RAGE.

stinging hornets behind my eyes
slugs in my throat
bouncing crickets in my gut
worms crawling under my skin

it settles
solidifying
a boulder rumbling around
hitting the walls of my mind
peutrid
festering
turning to guilt

With every mistake I make,
I'll carry this with me

YOU USED TO LOVE JOHNNY CASH

none of us knew why
but when you heard
ring of fire
you instantly calmed

such a silly little boy

I see this video of your grandpa rocking you,
singing you old country tunes
and you coo back

I wonder if your soul recognizes these songs
Is that why you sing along?

GRABBING MY FINGER

shove it in your mouth
start chewing

you don't have teeth yet
my darling little angel
but you're biting down on my finger like
your gums depend on it

> *Can you not bite me?*
> my younger self says with a laugh

You idiot
I think to myself

I wish I could go back
I would let you nibble on my fingers
all day long

anything
to get back those
precious little moments
of you snuggled on my chest

EYE ROLL

that's what I notice in this one
you're 2 months old here

that same sass has lived strong since
day 1
and I love you for it

I hope you never lose that fire
hope you protect the ones you love
hope you'll burn down any path
that dare block you

and I hope
you never
feel the darkness
I feel

GASPING

I hear it right away
the way your
wheezy little throat
gasps for air

I knew then
that there was something wrong
tried to tell your idiot pediatrician
and she said nothing was wrong

told me I was crazy
I don't need someone saying that
I already tell myself that
24/7

I just need someone on my side
need a doctor for you
that will listen to me when I say
I think there's something wrong

For weeks
they'll say you're fine
but one day

they'll learn
that I was right

You can't have dairy
that's nothing too scary
but they didn't believe me

Society needs
to believe its mothers
when we say
that something is wrong

MECHANICAL ROCKER

I see you sitting in that thing
the little chair that
rocks you back and forth

I'm sitting on the couch
watching TV
I know that I was probably just taking
a much needed break

But when I see that video
of your little smile
squirming in that stupid chair

I get angry with myself
Why did I let you sit in that
when my arms were free?

Why did I let you sit alone
when you didn't need to be?

I wish I could rewind time
wish I could go back
and restart the clock

of your childhood

Wish I could go back and
snuggle you better
harder
with more love

It's not that I didn't love you
but I know
deep down
I could've done better

THE WAY YOU LOOK AT HIM

and the way he looks at you
father and son
making faces at each other
such love
such adoration

you're a daddy's boy
through and through

makes me wonder
what I did wrong
to not make you
a momma's boy

MY SALVATION

the cure to this darkness
lies in the warmth
of your smile

THERE'S THIS SONG

the melodic tunes
are like
a soft caress
on my brain

I cling to the lyrics
like my life depends on it

listen to it for hours
on repeat

turning in circles
in the kitchen
my baby in my arms

trying to dance away
the fear
that plays through
my mind
like a loudspeaker

a siren telling me
I'm in danger
when the only danger
I'm in
is in my own mind

~ *dizzy on the comedown*

MY HEART

can be a beautiful place to land
I can love
so deeply
it scares me
a safe haven for all

But my mind
a padded cell
disguised
as creativity and
detailed plans

when really
it's just me
over analyzing everything
thinking of creative
new ways
to keep the tides
from pulling me under

DAYCARE

no one tells you
how scary it'll be
to leave your baby
with strangers

even when it's family
watching your tiny miracle
you'll still worry they will hurt him

THE FIRST DAYS BACK

at first felt like a breeze
a welcomed relief after 6 weeks
of being stuck inside
nowhere to hide
from my own mind

But after a day or so
I'll wish I was home
wish I could
hold my baby
in my arms
for just a few minutes longer
before walking out the door
feeling like I'm abandoning
the little miracle I made
to be watched by
someone
I worry
won't love him
as much
as I do

MY BEST FRIEND IS A SUPER MOM

she makes motherhood look easy
she posts on facebook all the time

Happy faces
words of adoration
cute photos with aesthetic outfits
socks that match
a house that's clean
always smiling

but one day
months from now

we'll sit together
and finally *talk*

She'll confess how hard it's been on her
we'll cry together
realizing that we both
fought the same battle
in silence

Mommas,
talk to your friends
tell them when you're drowning

Don't let your people think you're okay
you might just save their life
while they also save yours

THE TIME WHEN THEY START GETTING FUN

that's how my husband puts it
the first few weeks are easy
in theory, of course

they eat
sleep
poop
repeat
oh, and also cry

But eventually they get *'fun'*
they are more aware
more interactive

I've loved you at every stage
but now that you realize I'm a person
I'm more nervous than ever
that you'll realize
how terrified I am
to mess you up

YOUR FACE

is starting to change
you've grown into that round little nose

your cheek are still chunky
but I see the way it's changing

you're looking less like a newborn
and more like a baby

compared to your toddler face now
I'm surprised I even recognize you

But one thing that's stayed the same
is the icy blue of your daddy's eyes
you got them from him
and every time I look into them
I know what the meaning
of true love is

HIS HANDS AND FEET

work a little better now
he's a few months old
and instead of flailing around wildly
they actually grab on
he holds his feet and brings them to his mouth
all the while smiling
and babbling
god how my heart aches missing those days

THE DREADED BABY MONITOR

that time comes
when you realize that it's better for your baby
to sleep on their own

We move you into your nursery
and for once you sleep through the night

Am I the reason you woke so often?
Did I keep you awake at night?

But now,
the only connection I have to you
is through this fuzzy little monitor

I can't reach out
and touch you
make sure you're breathing
make sure you're alive

How will I get through the night?
and then a panic wakes me when it's 6 am
and I realize you never woke up last night

Not because you're hurt
or not breathing
but because you slept

You...
slept?
All night?

That moment of relief, of pure happiness
makes me realize
maybe this motherhood thing isn't so bad

MILESTONES

Who knew that the most exciting part of my day
would be watching you
learn to flip over on your tummy
one step closer
to needing me a little less

YOUR FIRST ROADTRIP

I don't even really remember

If I didn't have this video,
I don't think I'd recall at all

I remember you doing well in the car
You always have
You're the best travel buddy a mommy could wish for

In this one,
you're getting antsy
you're fussing and grumbling
until I make funny faces, of course

I think I'd do anything to make you smile

MY FIRST TRIP WITHOUT YOU

What a nightmare that was
I needed my partner
more than I wanted to admit

just me and the baby
"my family will help."

But what happens when
I can't fathom asking for it?

I don't realize how much I need you,
sometimes I worry you'll think I take your for granted
there won't ever come a day
where this baby and I
can live without you

Please,
never leave me

Thank you
~ *your stressed wife*

I SORT OF REMEMBER THIS TRIP NOW

Slowly memories come back
We went to a bridal shower out of state
my first solo-parenting ever
harder than I anticipated

I remember a woman
admiring my little boy
sleeping soundly in his stroller
while the rest of us socialized
> *You're so lucky, momma!*
> *He's such a good sleeper*
> *What an easy baby!*

she didn't know the dagger
she dug into my back
the way I'd wonder
This is what an easy baby is like?

I couldn't possibly have another…

If this is easy
then I'm fucking screwed
Why does it feel so impossible
to survive the day?

THIS ONE I'LL DELETE

Why I recorded a video of
you laughing one minute,
screaming crying the next
I'll never know

What the fuck was I thinking?
Why does this exist?
Did I hurt you on accident?
Why didn't I pick you up right away?

Even as the months go on,
and motherhood gets lighter,
you'll still have days where you feel like a monster

SECONDS AND MINUTES GO BY

I count them
you're getting older,
you're getting more mobile
and now my eyes stay glued to the time

I hate to admit it,
the way I keep track

1 hour until a nap,
until a break,
until a rest
that won't stop until you're well past two

my mind will never stop racing
my heart will never stop pounding
my brain will never stop waiting
for that inevitable nap

Now that life is manageable again,
I miss you when you sleep
but back then,
god did I crave those moments to myself
and it haunts me to this day

because now as you sleep,
I look at pictures of you

current ones
old ones

and I wish I could go back
hold you again,
cuddle you again
comfort you again

but I can't

YOU'RE MORE THAN SIX MONTHS OLD

I have pictures of a freshly cleaned house

the truth is,
I probably wasn't cleaning much before now

those first few months
are just about survival

you won't have the time
or energy
or will
to focus on the cleanliness of your home

and that's okay

You don't have to figure it all out right way
trust me

Your baby will still love you
Your still a good mom

Your worth
is not tied to how clean your floors are

YOU'VE ALWAYS BEEN A WATER BABY

well, mostly

To see this video of you
tiny feet
in a tiny tub
kicking away happily

Your baths will turn
from small soakings
to full on tidal waves

But it's worth it to see you happy

A SCARCITY MENTALITY

is a tricky beast

For months now,
I've been hunting
desperate to find enough formula to feed you

Thankfully you're eating some solids now,
but it doesn't replace the need

Those moments where I worry I can't feed you,
I'm reminded that I'm a failure

Really just my boobs,
but I won't make that distinction just yet

I'll spend hundreds,
maybe thousands,
hoarding formula

Trying to stock up before the next wave
ff shortages hits
and the fear returns

I MET ANOTHER MOM

We talked about our babies
I told her I wished mine would sleep through the night

She said she liked waking up
said she got to spend more time with him that way
since she works all day

What's that like?
I don't know that I'll ever enjoy
waking up every 3 hours

I think you're a liar

A YEAR AND A HALF AFTER BIRTH

I'll find out
I hemorrhaged
bled enough to almost need a transfusion

Knowing I was so close to darkness
and no one told me
no one even bothered
to tell my husband

makes me want to march down to the hospital
and drown them in my anger

WHAT IF

I drop you?
> *I might*

What if I fall down the stairs while I hold you?
> *Let's hope not*

What if someone breaks in
kills me
and you're left all alone?
> *Lock your doors?*
> *I don't know...*

What if I whack your head on the car door?
> *I will*

What if I accidentally raise my voice at you?
> *I will*

What if I accidentally make you cry?
> *I will*

What if I fall asleep on the couch with you in my arms?
> *I will*

But what if I turn over and accidentally smother you?
>	*I won't*

What if you don't like me?
>	*You will*

What if my dog snaps at you?
>	*He will*

What if you don't sleep?
>	*You will*
>		*eventually*

What if I don't connect with you?
>	*I will*
>		*eventually*

What if I spend so much time crying
that I'll miss important moments?
>	*I will*

What if,
while I'm crying,
you cry with me and
then we both just sit there

unconsolable
> *We will*

What if I worry myself into depression?
> *I will*

What if I regret becoming a mother?
> *I will*
>> *(for only a short period of time)*

BUT WHAT IF

in all this worry
I learn to
>	*survive*

Learn to love
myself and you
my new body
which no longer belongs to just me

Learn to love you
the way you deserve

Learn to juggle all my new responsibilities

Learn to love the chaos
the constant noise
the constant stimulation
the constant judgement from those
that aren't worth my time
>	*Maybe I won't love that last one...*

learn to give more than I thought possible
even when my body is tired

and my mind can't go on

Will I learn to adore motherhood?

Most importantly
Learn to forgive myself for the things I didn't do while
I was drowning

> *I will*
>
> > *eventually*

And so will you,
mamma reading this

> *Give*
> *It*
> *Time*

SOMETIMES

the hardest thing to do
the bravest thing
most courageous thing you can do
will be to ask
for help

TO THE VOICE IN MY HEAD

that blares like an alarm
startles me awake in the middle of the night

to the voice in my head that asks:
Is he okay?
Is he breathing?

to the voice in my head that wonders:
will he like me as his mother?
will I love him as my son?
is he better off with another?

to the voice in my head
that constantly questions
could someone do this better than me?

to the voice in my head
that won't let me rest
won't let me relax unless I've done
all the tasks on my list

to the voice in my head
that tells me I'm failing

before I've ever even been given
a chance to start

to the voice in my head
that says society is judging me
for the way in which I'm drowning

to the voice in my head
that convinces me other moms
aren't struggling as much as I am

to the voice in my head
that makes tears feel like
tidal waves

Kindly,
Fuck you

~ a new, rational voice
trying to claw her way to the surface

I FEEL LIKE

at this point I'm just telling stories
but that's motherhood

the first few months are hell
and then you learn to enjoy it

little by little
day by day
life gets easier
and suddenly

you can enjoy this new life you've built

Give it some time, momma
it won't always feel like you're drowning

YOU'RE PROBABLY THINKING

There's no way motherhood
is THIS hard
It probably isn't

I've seen perfection online
seen the women who
make everything homemade
breastfeed until their babies are well past the
"normal" stage

I've seen them
making homemade bread
and homemade baby food

Each day a cute outfit
matching with their babies

Going out into the world
seeing friends
seeing family

I see their perfection
and it cuts to my core

Why am I not like them?

New moms,
hear me.

Don't watch those videos
they're a small snippet
in a sea of possibilities

Your world
might not look like theirs
and that's okay

You don't have to breastfeed
You don't have to make your own baby food
You don't have to have dinner on the table
for when your partner comes home

and to you working mommas
you don't even have to cook tonight

If you need a sign
that you're enough
that you're doing enough
this is it

You being loving
nurturing
caring
patient
is more important
than the laundry or the dishes

When they're older

they won't remember how clean the house was
they won't remember if their pizza dough was homemade
they won't remember that every pair of socks matched

they'll remember that you loved them
they'll remember that you played with them
they'll remember that you held them
comforted them

That's all that matters

MONTHS LATER

it'll still feel like you're drowning
but that first night of sleep
will have you feeling like
you could take on the whole world

It's amazing what some rest can do
you'll still grieve
you'll still miss the old you
you might even still cry

I know I did

But hopefully
just maybe
that little morsel of dread
that you once felt
that voice that sang
    "When will I get my life back?"

Hopefully
for your sake
she'll shut the fuck up
and let you enjoy motherhood finally

ONE DAY

you'll wake up
the voice in your head
that little gnat driving you crazy

She'll be silent
Okay...
maybe she won't be entirely still
but she'll be quiet enough

Each day
you'll wake up and
you'll hear her a little less
and a little less
and then one day

Silence

Your mind may one day find peace
Your heart will one day settle
You'll finally catch your breath

One day

REPEAT AFTER ME:

I am not a bad mom
I am exactly what my child needs

Repeat it again
and again
and again

Until it becomes the anthem of your life
Until it's the song stuck in your head
Until your heart bleeds worth
Until your eyes cry acceptance
Until your mind finally settles

Once more for good measure:
I am not a bad mom
I am exactly what my child needs

GRANDPARENTS ARE A BLESSING

I don't know how I would've made it without them

I see the way they love you
see the way their worlds light up when you're near

All this time I've loved you
but there's something special
about the bond between grandbabies and our own
parents

MY DAD TELLS ME

that to love his grandbaby
is to love me all over again

I wonder if it's like a reset button

Do you think back to those early days
of trying to figure this shit out?

Do you feel like you get a second chance
to love again?

Do you wish things had been different
when I was little?

They didn't need to be,
let's be very clear

But sometimes I wonder
what kind of grandmother I will be

TO THE FRIEND WHO HAD A BABY FIRST

I'm sorry I didn't check in on your more
I'm sorry I didn't bring you dinners
I'm sorry I didn't pop in with coffee at random
to see how you were doing

I'm sorry I didn't text you more
I'm sorry I gave you so much space
I'm sorry you entered motherhood alone
I'm sorry I wasn't a better friend

I'm sorry.

LOVE CHANGES

after you've had kids

It's not spontaneous outings
or date nights at fancy restaurants
or late nights on the pier
or flowers and chocolates

It's getting the baby so your partner can sleep
It's doing the dishes
Vacuuming
Rubbing their back

Reminding them that they're enough
That they're valued

When you start to feel
more like roommates than lovers,
remember to communicate

find solace in each other's arms
offer just as much love to each other
as you do to the little bundle
you created together

Let them know that
when you look in your child's eyes
you see their warmth

Tell them that you see how hard they're working
and appreciate every little thing they do

That goes to moms and dads
it doesn't matter who you are in the relationship
don't forget
to cherish each other

IN THE BEGINNING

I will resent him
the man who helped me create
this beautiful little miracle

I'll be jealous
because his body didn't crack open
and bleed out her insides
his mind
did shatter with every overbearing thought

I'll wonder why fatherhood
seemed so much easier for him
How do I learn to transition
rather than digging in my heals
kicking and screaming
for what my life used to be?

Two years later
I'll realize how unfair that was
How cruel it was for my to think
that this new life wasn't hard on him too

He's watched me hurt
Watched me cry
Watched me weep without knowing how to help

He's had to let go of just as much freedom as I have
Had to watch the days
Where the baby cries too
And all he wants it momma

THERE'S A PHASE OF LOVE

where you have to relearn
what makes the other person
the one you want to spend your life with

Parenthood changes you
and through those changes
you'll learn to love your partner
more than you ever thought possible

Because you'll see them
in your child's eyes
your child's smile
all the things you love about them
you'll see in that sweet little baby

DON'T WISH THE YEARS AWAY

I know it's hard not to

You see other kids
talking, playing, interacting
You think to yourself:
> *I can't wait for my baby to do that*

to be more manageable
independent

But the truth it,
you'll wake up in two years like me
and you'll realize that while you wished away the years
they slipped through your fingertips

You woke up one day and he needed you a little less
didn't need you to help him in his chair
didn't need you to spoon feed him
didn't want you to brush his hair
didn't ask you to bring him a snack

Every second that we wish away their childhood,
thinking of easier times,
we risk losing these little moments

the tiny fingers grasped firmly around our own
the slump on your shoulder,
clinging to you like life itself
the squeals of joy when you come home

So don't wish these years away
I know they're hard
but you'll miss them some day

DEAR SOCIETY,

I'm not sure you understand
new moms
when we come to you
struggling
trying to survive
you give us shame
you foster guilt

You chose to be a mother
You chose to get pregnant
You chose this life

You're right, I did
But no one prepared me
for the lack of concern

You check in on new mothers
during the first few weeks

But you left them flounder every month after

You bring hot meals
offer to let us nap

offer to clean our homes
come over and take the baby from our arms

But all of that goes away
   "it's been months,
   you should be adjusted by now"

That may be true for some,
but others...

that's when we need you most

WORKING MOMS

The hardest part
is seeing the pictures and videos
sent to you
with good intentions

Your little man is doing great!
In your mind you wonder,
Without me?

At this point,
that nagging voice is much quieter
but she still rears her ugly head sometimes

When I see you
wearing a goofy hat,
playing with my best friend's little boy
not much older than you

I worry I'm not entertaining you enough
maybe I'm not as fun
but by now, I have a new voice in my head

They're starting to compete

fighting custody battles every day
a counter to my pessimism

Maybe I just need to learn
how to adjust my mentality
and then I'll realize

I'm doing better than I think

SOLIDS

If there's one thing I remember fondly
it's letting you try solids
seeing your face
squirm and fuss
All you've had to this point is sweet milky something or other
And now I offer you...

Broccoli

I know...
I'm sorry son
Sorry I let your first food be a leafy green

They told me if
I let you try fruits first
You'd always have a sweet tooth
If you're anything like me
There won't be anything in this world
That can change that

But for now,
I'll watch the videos
Giggle along with a younger me
as your get upset
that I would dare
offer you
anything but milk

TINY TOES

In this video
I'm tickling
those itty bitty little nubs
your chunky little feet
are the cutest thing I've seen
since that very first smile

SOMETIMES

I'm embarrassed to admit I'm writing this
ashamed of the way I struggled in the beginning

Now,
I hope it helps someone
makes someone feel seen
shows them they're not alone

I still worry,
I'm giving bad advice
or painting a bad picture of motherhood

I hope you know being a mom is incredible
but it's the hardest thing I've ever had to do

MOURNING

I wish someone would have told me
how much I would mourn who I was

Mourn the freedom I once had
Mourn sleeping in
Mourn my hobbies
Mourn my friends
Mourn my old life

But I also wish
someone would have told me
how much I would celebrate

There is so much joy
in this marathon called motherhood

Your baby's first smile
Their first crawl
First steps
First words

The first night they sleep the whole way through
(That one you'll throw an actual party for)

So many focus on the mourning
What you loose
I promise,
You'll find joy again

The first month is hard
But I swear to you,

You'll find joy in the hardships
Companionship in the loneliness
You will learn to love your new life
Just give it time

HIS FIRST TRIP TO THE BEACH

This memory
I do remember

How could I forget
The complete and utter disgust
on your face
when I put you in that water

What's funny is that
you'll come to crave the water
it'll be hard for me to keep you out of it
when you're a toddler

But as a baby,
Boy you sure look like you're judging me

YOU SMILE SO MUCH NOW

it used to be
that you cried more than you smiled

That's the beautiful thing about you getting older
I wish I could do back to
the newborn stage sometimes

Love you a little harder
Love you with more patience
Love you till the waves that
threatened to drown me didn't matter

But nothing compares to
this new version of you

The one that smiles when you see me
smiles when you see your daddy
notices that we have dogs
loves the colorful blocks and books

You're so inquisitive now
and while I miss the worm you once were,

I realize
That somehow my heart keeps growing

And every second you get older,
my love somehow expands

And now the waves that are drowning me feel
more like love that's consuming me
maybe the waters are slowly drying up

FATHER'S DAY

I see the pictures
of your daddy
holding you high and proud
his first father's day
all for him

We do everything he wants
honor him
for the amazing daddy he is

The provider
The giver
The one helping
to keep me afloat

WE'RE LUCKY

You have a daddy that loves us
I hear horror stories
of men who
let their women drown
without a care in the world
for their wellbeing
who don't even change diapers

Lucky doesn't begin to describe it

MOMS

are never in pictures
or videos

It's always dads
or siblings
or grandparents
but never moms

Somehow everyone always forgets about us
forgets we need proof of
a version of ourselves
that will forget how much we did
how hard we loved

We'll forget it all
and need proof that we were
a decent mother

Families,
Please take picture and videos
of new moms
She'll cling to them one day

YOU'LL MISS HER

This version of you
The one that's struggling

It might seem strange
to miss a version
delirious from lack of sleep
weeping from wrecking hormones
overwhelmed by pain

But you'll miss her

You'll envy the time she had
The baby cuddles
The days spent holding that precious little miracle

I would live it all again
The pain
The sorrow
The fear
The anxiety

I would live it all again to hold
those little hands in my hands

those little toes between my fingers
to see those baby blue eyes
looking back at me,
sleepy and confused

I would live it all again
I would love it all again

YOU BOUNCE IN YOUR BOUNCER NOW

those same little feet
that used to do catapults off my ribs
now hit against the ground

You smile and laugh
hopping and jumping until you tire yourself out

To think you'll be jumping off of coffee tables a year later
hoping someone will catch you,

Time is an incredible thing
but it's also a thief

I HAD THIS DREAM

When I first woke up
I felt disturbed
But as I thought about it,
I understood its message

I dreamt that in every stage
From newborn to baby
Baby to toddler
Our children didn't grow
They merely duplicated

What ensued was chaos
Overwhelm
Frustration
Lots and lots of messes

But when I thought about it,
I realized it's quite true, isn't it?

Our children may get bigger
Grow older
Need us a little less each day

But they'll never stop being our baby
The one we brought home from the hospital

They may be a big toddler now,
But that doesn't mean there isn't a newborn inside
That needs hugs and unconditional love

They grow bigger
Get bolder
Need us less and less

But they'll always be that same squirmy newborn
That kept us up late at night
Made us cry ourselves to sleep sometimes
Made our hearts explode when we saw their first smile

They'll always be
Perfect

THINK OF IT THIS WAY

Your child
doesn't have anything to compare you to
They've never had another mother
who cried less
did the dishes more
kept a cleaner home

This is all they know
We can't beat ourselves up,
comparing ourselves to other women

When will we realize that
we're not competing
we're in this together

MILESTONES

No one warns you
the way in which milestones vary

We think they're one size fits all
but they're not

My boy won't hit all his milestones on time
and the pediatrician will make me worry
but he's got time

Don't worry, mamma
Your baby is okay
Even if they're just a little bit behind their peers

MOMS NEED OTHER MOMS

that of which I'm sure

Like mammals need air to breathe
Fish need water
Plants need the sun

We need other moms
not just for friends for our babies

But to feel seen
to be honest
to admit how much we're struggling
so we can lift each other up
and remind one another
that we are not alone

They say it takes a village
that's very true
find your village
and be honest with them

You'll be surprised how many are just like you

JUST WAIT

They say

Just wait till they start crawling
You'll never get them to stop moving

Just wait till they start walking
You'll never sit down again

Just wait till they start talking
You'll never have a quiet moment again

Just wait till they turn two
You'll never have a moment of peace

Just wait till they turn three
You'll never stop arguing with the little version of you

Just wait till they turn four
You'll lose them to preschool

Just wait till they turn five
You'll lose them to kindergarten

Just wait till they turn sixteen
You'll never see them because they'll be out
running the town

Just wait till they move out
Get married
Have their own kids

Just wait.

I wish people would stop telling you
to just wait

How about instead
You just wait...

For their first smile
Their first laugh

Their first crawl
Their first step
Their first run
Their first tumble
Their first scraped knee

Their first full night of sleep

Their first bite of food
Their first time trying your favorite dessert

Their first time making a friend
Their first time showing empathy
Their first movie

Their first time reading a word
Their first time recognizing a color

It keeps going
There's so many things to look forward to

Just wait and you'll see

YOUR BEST FRIEND

There's a special bond
Between your best friend
And your own kid

They will love them like their own
Love them like they're blood

Treat them like their own child

Watching your child
be loved so deeply
by someone who has no obligation to love them
heals a part of you
that you didn't know was broken

LOVE

to hold the world in your hands
to see the essence of it before your eyes
to find meaning in a smile
a coo
a flutter of eyelashes over sleepy eyes

That is the triumph of motherhood
It's the most traumatic of miracles
you'll ever experience

MOMMA'S GOTCHA

When the world feels too big
When you cry and feel lost

Momma's gotcha
When those little hands
Feel empty and want someone to hold

Momma's gotcha
When everything feels too much
Too big
Too loud
Too scary

Momma's gotcha
When your legs begin to wobble
When your amateur feet
Don't know how to hold you

Momma's gotcha
When your skin breaks
And her heart hurts to see you bleed

Momma's gotcha
When the world feels scary
When you're somewhere new and
You won't know who to trust

Momma's gotcha
When your body hurts
From growing
And your mind spins from developing

Momma will always have your back

YOU'RE 2 ½

You need us less and less
You say no
You're just realizing you're a whole person
Capable of being defiant

Yes, you're very **very** defiant
But you're also loving

You're sunshine
You're electricity
You're a star speckled sky
You're the cool breeze on a hot summer's day
You're wild
And I love you for it

I DON'T CALL MYSELF A POET

When I tell others about this book
Instead I call this
Word vomit
Emotion soup
A raw manifesto of love and sacrifice

Never have I ever
Been so overwhelmed by joy and sorrow
Without even knowing it
I've helped myself heal
Just by writing down the jumble
Of what I've been feeling for
The last two years

TWO YEARS DROWING, YES

But also
Two years afloat

Two years learning to swim with my demons
Two years learning to love
harder than I thought possible

Two years finding the light in my darkness
Two years learning to take care of myself
(most of the time)

Two years appreciating the miracle we made
Two years learning to pour from an empty cup

Two years...

Two years?

I blinked and suddenly
That time has vanished

THERE ARE DAYS

Where you will pour from an empty cup
You will give more than you knew possible
You will feel like you have nothing left
But you will continue on
Because that little life
The one you love so dearly
Needs you

MY MOM CALLS

I sent a video of you
Sliding down a slide
It's wet at the bottom
You splash through the puddle
Take a tumble at the bottom
We laugh
You get back up
Run to do it all again

She loves that video of you
Tells me
watching it was healing
tells me stories of her childhood
that ensure I don't ever
want to talk to her father again

Maybe I'm not doing as bad as I thought

What I wouldn't give
to open her chest
take out that tiny toddler in her soul
and cuddle her
like I cuddle you

What I wouldn't give
to fix the wrongs of her past

to try giving her a better childhood
a childhood like I had
(she worries she did a bad job)

she didn't
but we all worry,
don't we?

MY FRIEND TELLS ME

If he's half the person I love
in the whole wide world
and half me

then the parts of me
I'm scared of
or don't like
can't be that bad

Because he's still got
a whole lot of love
from his dad inside

Maybe I'm not all that bad either

TO THE FRIENDS WHO STOPPED TEXTING BACK

The ones who don't have kids
who don't care to be around
the crying and diapers

I get it

I'll resent you for it,
Blame myself
Wonder what I could've done
To make you stay around

But I get it

I'm not the same person you became friends with
Motherhood will ensure you lose those not meant for you
But you'll find some amazing new people, too

I do miss you
I just wish you'd stayed

WHY ARE YOU CRYING M-MA?

Because you don't fit in your newborn clothes anymore
Because you don't want me to swaddle you anymore
Because you don't fit across my chest anymore

Why are you crying, mama?
Because you can sit on your own now
Because you'd rather walk than be carried
Because I put you to bed in your crib for the last time
Without even realizing it

Why are you crying, mommy?
Because you don't want to hold my hand anymore
Because you won't let me carry you to bed anymore
You walk yourself now

Ugh, why are you crying, mom?
Because you'll want to hang out with your friends
Rather than your nostalgic mom
Because one day you'll want to get a drivers license all
of a sudden
Even though the thought used to scare you
Because you'll graduate one day

Why are you crying, mom?
Because you'll get married one day
Because one day I'll hold your babies in my arm
And remember what you were like when you were little

Why am I crying?
Because one day
Everything becomes the last day

I'M CONVINCED THAT

For the sake of mankind's existence
and the continuation of our species
there's a sort of reset button
seated somewhere in our brains
a little switch that makes us forget

the pain of childbirth
the delirium of exhaustion
the loneliness of those early days

there's no way we've survived this long
without some sort of divine intervention

OUR ANCESTORS HAD IT RIGHT

It takes a village
to raise a child

But what happens
When the village doesn't call?
When the village stops checking in?

When the village invites you out for drinks every Friday night
like they forgot you have a whole other life to care for

When the village invites you but not the baby
forgetting you're a package deal

When the village doesn't accept
that it takes you longer to respond sometimes

When the village doesn't understand why you're so tired all the time
When the village doesn't get why you're so sad
So lonely

They've been inviting you everywhere
Why do you feel so alone?

It's take a village
But sometimes your village has to change

You have to go out
and find new people

Walk up to every mom with a child and ask
to be friends

Moms need other moms
like flowers need air and water and sunlight
like the waves need the moon for their tides
like our lives depend on it
Because they do

Find your village
Accept that your village
won't look the same as it did before

Forgive them for abandoning you
They'll get it if they ever have kids one day

I'M NOT RELIGIOUS

But I see god in your smile
I see fate in the creases next to your eyes
I recognize the universe in the curls of your hair
I hear angels in the way you laugh
I meet destiny every time your hand grasps mine

I'm not religious
but being your momma made me
finally see
life as it could be

WHEN HE WAS BORN

His eyes were a deep blue
As deep as the sadness I felt in my chest

As he's gotten older
and the heartache has lessened
His eyes have grown lighter
and now at almost 3
they're blue and brown and green
as if every lesson I've learned
has been woven into the fabric of his being

WHEN I LOOK AT YOU

I see every version of you

The newborn
Sleepless nights
Explosive diapers
Sleepy cuddles

The infant
Learning to control your hands
Learning to kick your feet
Seeing more and more of the world

The mobile baby
Inching your way across the floor
Stumbling as you pull yourself up
Fumbling as you try to figure out how your feet work

The toddler
Who refuses to eat what I make him
Who tells me no
Who gives the best hugs

I see each version of you
Always
No matter how old you are,
Those versions of you will always exist

CALMER WAVES

SHORTLY AFTER 2

We find out we're having another boy

Panic washed over me
This wasn't planned
This couldn't possibly be

But fate doesn't care if you're ready
She throws things at you
Tells you to take it slow
And steady

You may not be ready
But you'll get there
Just wait

So while I dig in my heels
Trying to stop the tides from turning

I'll just have to keep reminding myself
That I've endured

Despite the constant raging burning
Despite the overwhelming waves that drowned me

Despite the fact that motherhood feels
like someone peeling back every layer
to expose the darkest parts of myself

Fate tells me to settle
I was born to be your mamma
I'll see it one day
But for now,
I'll just heal

Get ready for life's miracles
and pray
that somehow, someway

It'll all be okay in the end

A NURSE

during my second pregnancy
tells me that
any act taking care of myself
inadvertently takes care of my child too
because I can't be everything he needs
if I'm not cared for, too

She doesn't know
how much this changed my view

Now when I do things for myself,
I play her words
like an anthem
draw a heart on the shower door
like a ritual of self-love
because even something as simple
as a shower
can make you feel human again

NOT LONG AFTER

we welcome your baby brother
I worry you'll feel abandoned
less loved
replaced

I think any mother feels that way
It makes me hold you a little closer
Love you a little harder
Not want to let go

I see the way you look
when visitors come to see us
and the first thing they do
is say hi to the baby

You look so defeated
it breaks my heart to see you sad
so instead I'll tell them
    say hi to big brother first
And that will help soothe the hurt
for just a little while

I WORRIED YOU'D HATE HIM

for taking our attention from you
but you've opened your heart to him

The moment you saw him
you loved him
nearly as much as I've loved you

I can't help but wonder
where that comes from

Did you see it between your dad and I?
Do you love so fiercely because
it's the same love
that created you?
sustained you?
kept you alive the last two years?
kept your mommy alive the last two years?

Maybe I didn't do as bad of a job as I think I did
if this is how hard you'll love
your baby brother

A CONVERSATION ON GUILT

I feel guilty...
like my son deserves a better mom
like he'll resent me
for how much I struggled

I feel guilty...
because things are so much easier
the second time around
Motherhood comes more natural this time,
and I'm not drowning as quickly

I feel guilty...
because I worry
that my first
will forever hate me
because I couldn't be everything he deserved

    My friend asks me:
    Is it your fault?

What do you mean?

    Did you choose to be depressed?

Well...no
Now that I think of it
I didn't

    Guilt implies
    that something is your fault
    that you chose that for yourself

    Depression isn't your fault
    you can't control it

    You should never feel guilty
    about the way in which you survived
    when you were drowning

    You did the best you could
    with what you could give

and that is all your baby needs

EVERYTHING FEELS

faster the second time around

I blinked and he's 4 months old

I blinked and he's tripled his birth weight

I'll blink and soon he'll be crawling
walking, jumping
causing havoc alongside his brother

Why do the days feel so long
Yet the months and years

go by without warning?

I THINK WE ALL WORRY

We're terrible mothers
I'm starting to realize
There's love in that worry
If we didn't care
We wouldn't fear
We're all doing better than we think
~ almost 3 years postpartum

I TOLD MYSELF

I wouldn't be one of those parents
that lets their kid have screen time
lol...
look at me now

MY BIRTH PLAN?

Show up
Have the baby
Don't scream too loud
Make my husband order sushi after

BEING PREGNANT AGAIN

I'll spend so much time worrying
that the darkness will consume me like last time
that the tide will once again pull me under

I'll spend so much time worrying
I won't even take pictures of this pregnancy
of this baby bump

And then when he's out
and the waves are calmer than I expected
I won't have photos to look back on
and I'll be sad for a different reason

TELLING MY MOM ABOUT #2

She'll cry
not tears of joy,
but of worry

She's excited, yes
but she remembers how I was
after baby #1

She was helpless
drowning right alongside me
I supposed the worry
never really goes away
no matter how old your babies are

THERE IS NOTHING MORE PURE

Than the love my oldest
Shows his little brother

MOST DAYS

I still pray for naptime
Worship it like it's a god
That little bit of alone time

Some days,
He won't take a nap now
It's been almost three years
And I still count the clock some days

But I've learned that it's okay to need a break
I've learned it's okay to ask for one,
Without needing to feel guilty

YOU'LL THINK FOR A WHILE

that you lost your freedom
but the truth is
you'll find a new version of it

A baby will show you the freedom of rest
while you may feel like you have a million things to do
you will be forced to take time for yourself
or you'll drown

A toddler will show you freedom in slowing down
       (and sometimes speeding up!)
they'll want to stop to examine the world
look at rocks on the ground
watch how they ripple in puddles
realizing that bugs exist
and a whole new world opens up to them

A child will show you freedom in being curious
in asking questions
allowing their curiosity to grow
and finding a safe space
a solid foundation
for exploration

A teenager will show you freedom in independence
in the way they try to rebel
in big and small actions
in the funny way
they try to lie
thinking you won't realize it

A young adult will show you freedom once again
in curiosity
trying to determine who they are
finding their people
finding their love
finding their purpose

If you're lucky enough
You'll get a front row seat in every stage of life
Until one day
Little voices get to call you grandma this time

The years...
they'll force you to slow down
and you'll find freedom in the things that
growing up stole from you

You'll cloud gaze again
Look up at the stars
Realize how small we are
You'll pick dandelions and
Hunt for four leaf clovers
You'll find friendship in bees and
Make up stories about fairies

You'll find freedom again
It just won't look the way it used to

WHILE THE WORLD SLEEPS

She waits
Counts the seconds
The minutes
Watches them pass
Calculates down to the hour
How much sleep will sustain her tomorrow

While the world sleeps,
She watches
Memorizes the profile
Of what love created
Observes the flutter of lashes
Over sleepy eyes

While the world sleeps,
She thinks
This is what motherhood can be like
And with a grateful heart
Goes back to sleep

MOTHERHOOD

Doesn't seem scary this time
Maybe because I've already been doing it for two years

Motherhood
Doesn't have to be scary this time
Maybe because my brain isn't my enemy now
    (most of the time)

Motherhood
Is beautiful at last
Maybe because I'm learning to
Recognize my blessings
Register my heart for what it is
Not just an anxious mess
But a loving mess
Protective
Fierce
    (a little tired)
But loving with so much force
it can shatter the waves this time

Motherhood
I think I understand you now

HAVING A SECOND

Makes me realize how much I've forgotten
Postpartum depression
is a thief
just like time is a thief

So many little details
Derailed and stolen
My heart aches for my first born's early days
I wish I could have a second chance

A do-over
To do better for him
But it's already been three years...
And there are no reset buttons in life

NOTHING HURTS MORE

than seeing others
annoyed with your child

Our friends' older kids come over
they don't want to play with the toddler who
is bossy and territorial of toys
who only seems to say no

He doesn't understand yet
how to be a friend
and they don't bother to teach him

It'll break something inside you
drudge up old memories
but at least he has his momma

SITTING ON THE COUCH

I memorize him
My second son
I know how fleeting these days are
I'll blink and this moment will be gone
He'll be older
Won't need me anymore

So I'll study his features
The curl on his forehead
The slope of his nose
The cowlick at the back of his head
The green blue of his eyes
The eyes of his daddy
The tiny fingers tapping away
The toes he tries to stick in my face
The cackle afterwords
The love

That is one thing postpartum depression
can never take away

THE SECOND WASN'T PLANNED

But holding him
Seeing that smile
I know that fate must be real
Because I was born to be your momma
And I didn't realize it before
But my family wasn't whole until you joined us

All's right with the world

I USED TO CRAVE BEING ALONE

longed for peace,
for quiet
wanted so desperately
to not have to talk to anyone
that I'd hide away and
not speak to anyone as long as
I could avoid it

Motherhood changed that for me
I no longer crave being alone
When I am,
I only feel emptiness
A gaping hole where my village lies

Motherhood forced me to step outside my comfort zone
made me realize,
It's okay to ask for help
It's okay to want to be around others
It's okay to talk to strangers
It's okay to crave friendship from other moms

I don't want to be alone anymore
I don't want to hide away anymore
I don't want to look at myself in the mirror, and wonder
who the hell is staring back

I want to get to know myself again
Learn about my hobbies
My interests
Rediscover long forgotten dreams
Brush the dirt off of them and tell them,
> *You're allowed to exist*
> *You're allowed to be wanted*
> *You're needed*

Motherhood took so much away
Yet reminded me who I actually was
It's stripped me down to bare bones
Removed the excess and only left
What's good for me
What's right for me

I'm not just learning to swim,
I'm meeting myself all over again
I'm learning to be me

THROUGH MOTHERHOOD

You'll meet your demons
If you're lucky
If you let them in
You'll get to know them
Rather than drown in the waves
You'll pull up a pool floaty
Learn to go with the flow
Maybe enjoy a margarita along the way

FLAMINGOS

When they become mothers
Lose their color
They spend so much energy
Ensuring their babies thrive

It's poetic, don't you think?
The thing that makes them recognizable
Their pink feathers and vibrant nature
It fades

We are flamingos, too
But we don't have to let motherhood steal our color

Instead,
I choose to embrace a new one

Before motherhood
I was green

Then I became blue
A sad sap stuck beneath the water
Kicking and screaming to go back to what she was

Now I'm teal
Or maybe yellow
I like the way those colors make me feel

They're vibrant and happy
Remind who I am now
The same but different
A whole new shade but no longer watery gray

ANOTHER MOM HOLDS MY BABY

Her boys are now 10 and 12
There's a sadness in her eyes
As she hold mine close to her heart
I see her look at her boys
I wonder what she's thinking
I bet she's missing them
Even though they're only a few feet away
> *They're growing up*
> *They barely need me*
Though she says it with confidence
She glances at my baby
And I realize how
Bittersweet
Motherhood is

If you do it right
Your children will be well-prepared
to live without you

But hopefully
If you do it right,
They'll still crave you in their life
The way this mother

Craves to hold a newborn
Wishing she could do back
And do it all again

IN THE HOSPITAL THE SECOND TIME

My little one spends days in the NICU
The nurses here for a paycheck
Just come in and take care of me
The ones who love their job
Come in,
Eyes searching
For the little bundle of joy they expect to see
In the arms of the new mommy
But there's no baby to see
My heart feels empty
Just as my arms feel purposeless
He was a part of me only days ago
And now he's gone
I know he's fine,
But he's not *here*
With me
Where he should be
How do I explain this loneliness
To someone who isn't a parent?

AT WORK

There's this long hallway
It's dark,
But the sunshine glows at the end
 Every day when I leave,
That hallway feels longer
Like I can't escape

It reminds me of motherhood sometimes
There are days that feel impossible
But eventually,
You reach the door
You meet the end of the hallway
And step through
You're no longer who you once were

A new 'you' appreciates the freedom
The light on the other side
You step out from darkness
And suddenly realize there's peace on the other end

I think I'm finally stepping through that door
~ 3 years postpartum

THERE'S A MOMENT

Before your baby is born
You scream and cry
Say
> *I can't do this!*
> *I can't do this!*

The pain becomes so overbearing
Soul-crushing
Like the anger of all the women who came before you
Finally releasing

But then your baby is in the world
And all at once,
The pain disappears

Relief will settle in your bones
You'll hold you bundle of joy
And all will be right with the world

MY SECOND IN THE NICU

The nurse comes to tell me,
We need breastmilk
Start pumping right away

It's not a question,
Not even a suggestion

It's a demand

The first time around,
I almost died from the pressure
I tell her to just give him formula
She doesn't take 'no' for an answer

My husband stands up for me
I don't even remember what he says
But I remember how I felt
To have someone on my side
To stand up for me
When I was at my most vulnerable

Husbands, partners, fathers, parents,
Stick up for the moms in your life

Like a bug petrified in stone,
Our voices may feel small
But you can advocate for us

WHATEVER YOU DO, DON'T BLINK

Your eyes will open and
you'll realize years have passed,
not just months or days

Don't blink,
because you'll realize your baby is losing
his chubby face
his features are morphing into a tiny man

You'll hardly recognize the little human staring back at you

Don't.
Blink.

BECOMING A MOTHER

Didn't just teach me about
raising boys
or protecting them
keeping them alive
when kids' natures seems to be
trying to hurt themselves constantly

It also showed me
The wounds I needed to heal
The inner child that needed love, too
In need of protection and support

Somewhere along the way,
Society made me feel like my words weren't worthy
And by writing this book and others

I feel like I'm not just taking care of myself
And my family
But also little-me

We finally wrote that book you've been
dreaming about
and countless others

THE PAIN OF EARLY MOTHERHOOD

Will wither away
Like the changing of the seasons

You'll exit the desolate winter
and find that
You're now in spring
The relationship with your baby
Is the tiny budding flowers
The pollen speckling the earth
Like your tears may sometimes settle on your cheeks
But this doesn't last forever

And as time goes on,
Those flowers will grow into summer
Your world will be in full bloom with joy

Just as crickets dance on a hot summer's day,
So will your baby
Just as the bees buzz from flower to flower,
So will your little one explore their new world
Just as the waves crash along the shoreline,
So will the love for your child

Fall will come too,
And the baby you held in your arms will
Turn to a toddler like the falling of leaves
He'll be scattered just as the debris is in a forest
But there will still be beauty
Just as the air chills
Signifying that summer is coming to an end
So will the changes of your child

You may go through a season of winter again
As you mourn the loss of your baby's younger self
But just as it goes every year,
Spring will come again

Your baby will become a toddler,
Then a child, and so on...
Until one day he's a man
Every season will bring highs and lows

But no matter what,
Spring will always come

I STARTED THIS BOOK A YEAR AGO

On the night of my son's second birthday

Now here I sit,
On the day of his third

In all the chaos of the last year,
I've learned a thing or two

I was drowning before, but
I find myself afloat

suddenly

My house is still a mess most days,
The place is never quiet
There's beautiful chaos
And sorrow,
Missing my baby for who he used to be

But I'm no longer drowning
I can finally look back at photos and videos
I still want to cry
I miss him when he was little

But my tears are summoned for different reasons

This last year,
I've thrived
Learned how to embrace motherhood
Versus digging in my heels,
Kicking and screaming

I've found peace
And gratitude
I've found freedom in reframing my view of the day

I've learned not to beat myself up every time
Something doesn't go my way

I've learned,
That life just isn't that serious

The stress and unhappiness I once felt
has been replaced by a lust for life

I want to live,
And dance,
And play,
And write poems about something happy

Motherhood,
I've embraced you at last
This is who I am now
And I'm wholeheartedly in *love* with her

So on the day of my son's third birthday,
I drop the anchor finally
I could probably tell stories forever
Instead, I can look forward

To the next phase,
The next version of these two boys
The next few years that'll probably fly by

Somehow in the making of this word vomit
Jumbled mess of raw emotions and sorrow
And love
So, so much love

I've finally
learned to swim

ACKNOWLEDGMENTS

I'd like to thank my family for helping me get through those tough early days. Thank you for taking the baby so I could sleep. (You'd be shocked how many problems can be solved by a nap!)

Thank you to my husband. Through all our ups and downs, you'll always be my best friend and biggest advocate.

Thank you to my friends who've supported me. To the ones who I've known since high school, and the ones I've met thanks to motherhood. I couldn't imagine going through life without my tribe.

Thank you to the poets who inspired me: Kwame Alexander, Jacqueline Woodson, Rupi Kaur, Whitney Hanson, and Jason Reynolds.

And thank you, reader. Thank you for going on this journey with me. If you're a struggling mom, just know it gets better.

I hope you, too, learn to swim.

ABOUT THE AUTHOR

JM Lee is a proud member of the LGBTQ+ community who writes the kind of heartfelt, authentic stories she wishes she'd had growing up. A teacher by day and a writer by passion, she hopes to inspire the next generation of storytellers to find their voice. When she's not chasing plot twists or wrangling her two energetic boys, you can find her rewatching Buffy the Vampire Slayer, belly dancing, or hanging upside down in an aerial yoga hammock.

MORE BY JM LEE

THE NOVUS PROPRIUS CHRONICLES
Young Adult Dystopian Fantasy written at 13
Revamp coming soon!

THE LONDINIUM SAGA
New Adult Gaslamp Fantasy
Curse of the Blood Queen
Prince of the Coral Throne
Coven of the Hunted (coming soon)

And more to come!
Follow me on instagram
@jmleebooks

or visit my website:
www.jmlee.info

www.ingramcontent.com/pod-product-compliance
Lightning Source LLC
LaVergne TN
LVHW030319070526
838199LV00069B/6508